# SPECIAL THINGS

"Think of something
you really like to do —
your *special* thing,"
the teacher said.
"You can tell your ideas
one by one. Then we'll
put them all in
a big class book."

Ted scratched his head.
"What *is* my special thing?"
he wondered.

Rita said she really liked acting.

But that didn't help Ted.
He still couldn't think of anything.

Lee said he really liked sailing.

But that didn't help Ted.
He'd never even been sailing.

Trish said she really liked fishing.

But that didn't help Ted.
He didn't like fishing at all.

Carl said he really liked
going to the museum.

But that didn't help Ted.
He liked going to the museum,
but not *that* much.

11

Claire said she really liked
climbing trees.

But that didn't help Ted, either.
He hated heights.

When it was Ted's turn,
he *still* couldn't think of anything.

But then the teacher said,
"Oh Ted, what wonderful pictures
for our book!"

And at last the class was ready
to make a *very* special book.